Church and World
in the New Testament

Church and World in the New Testament

Johannes Schneider

translated by
HENLEE H. BARNETTE *and*
WAYNE BARNETTE

MERCER UNIVERSITY PRESS ■ MACON, GEORGIA

ISBN 0-86554-063-2

This text is based on a lecture delivered by the author at the
Congress of Free Church Students in Göttingen, May 1955.

Published originally as *Gemeinde und Welt im Neuen Testament*
by Oncken Verlag, Wuppertal (1955), the English translation is by
arrangement with Oncken Verlag and is copyright © 1983 by
Mercer University Press, Macon GA, USA.

Library of Congress Cataloging in Publication Data

Schneider, Johannes, 1895-1970.
    Church and world in the New Testament.

    Translation of: Gemeinde und Welt im Neuen Testament.
    1. Church and the world. 2. Bible. N.T.—Criticism,
interpretation, etc. I. Title.
BR115.W6S27913 1983   261.1   82-25879
ISBN 0-86554-063-2

Table
of Contents

Translators' Preface

JOHANNES SCHNEIDER earned degrees from Göttingen and the University of Berlin, one in the field of political science and the other in theology. He taught New Testament at Breslau before becoming associate professor at the University of Berlin. From 1938-1939 he was visiting professor at Ottawa University in Ottawa, Kansas. Upon returning to Germany, he discovered the Nazis had dismissed him from the faculty at University of Berlin. He was restored to his professorship after the war in 1945. Later he was appointed Dean of the Theological Faculty of University of Berlin, the only Baptist in the divinity school.

Through the efforts of Dr. William A. Mueller, former professor at Eastern Baptist Seminary, Southern and New Orleans Baptist Seminaries, Dr. Schneider lectured in this country at Eastern Baptist Seminary in 1938 and at Southern Baptist Seminary in Louisville, Kentucky in 1951.

Dr. Schneider wrote numerous scholarly articles, including thirty-one articles for the *Theologisches Wörterbuch zum Neuen Testament*. He also wrote eighteen books, among them *Der*

Hebräerbrief, translated by Dr. Mueller and published under the title *The Letter to the Hebrews* (Eerdmans, 1957).

The problem of the relationship of the church to the world is a perennial one. Church-world confrontation has been the concern of the apostles, church fathers, the great reformers of the sixteenth century and by theologians from the post-Reformation era to the present. In this century a number of scholarly works on the church's relation to the world have appeared. Among these are: Ernst Troeltsch, *The Social Teaching of the Christian Churches* (1931); John Bennett, *Christian Ethics and Social Policy* (1946); C. J. Cadoux, *The Early Church and the World* (1955); H. Richard Niebuhr, *Christ and Culture* (1951); and Langdon Gilkey, *How the Church Can Minister to the World Without Losing Itself* (1964).

Schneider's small book, *Gemeinde und Welt im Neuen Testament,* is significant in that it presents the New Testament perspective on the church and world in confrontation. It focuses on how church and world are both opposed and related to each other. It includes individual treatments of church-state relations, husband-wife relations, parent-child relations, the Christian and earthly possessions, and the personal behavior of the Christian in the world.

Henlee H. Barnette
Wayne Barnette
Louisville and Nashville
1982

INTRODUCTION

❦

Church and World
in the New Testament

THE THEME "Church and World" is among the most important concerns of the church of Jesus. Although it has been dealt with often, it is frequently revitalized because the constantly changing world and the concrete situation in which we live continuously present us with new problems.

This text is meant to point out the guidelines given in the New Testament. For we can find solutions to the questions that confront us and mastery over the tasks before us only when we first have heard the sayings of Jesus and the apostles. The New Testament contains perceptions that serve as our standard and that are obligatory for our thoughts, our judgments, and our actions.

In order to master the large quantity of material, even to a slight extent, we will limit ourselves to four thesis-like propositions which will have to be developed in more detail.

Of course, we can only speak of the relationship between church and world if we have first stated briefly what is meant by "world" and "church" in the New Testament.

CHAPTER ONE

World and Church are in Opposition to Each Other

W‍E WILL DIVIDE the sayings of the New Testament concerning *the world* into four groups.

THE WORLD IS A WORLD CREATED BY GOD

God is the basis and the originator of the creation (Acts 17:24); he has called it into existence by his almighty word (Heb. 11:3). In this, as both the Gospel of John and the letters to the Colossians and the Hebrews (Col. 1:16; Heb. 1:2) attest, he has used Christ as the mediator of creation. Everything has been created through Christ and for him. As the "firstborn of creation" (Col. 1:16) he upholds the universe by his word of power (Heb. 1:3); everything that is has its existence in him (Col. 1:17). When the world was created, it was pure and good, and man was the image of God. The creation of the world is the first revelation of God—the manifestation of his eternal power and divine greatness, from which to this day the invisible nature of God can be perceived (Rom. 1:20).

THE WORLD IS MARKED BY ITS APOSTASY FROM GOD

Since the fall of man, all of creation has been subjected to the curse of transitoriness (Rom. 8:20). Mankind has lapsed into sin and death. Given to its worldliness, it is a world separated from God, secularized, and demonized—a world which, in its high-handedness, acts as if it is autonomous, but actually is under the lordship of satanic powers. Satan is the god of this aeon (2 Cor. 4:4). He blinds the minds of the unbelievers and causes decisions displeasing to God on the part of individuals and of secular potentates. The world, despite its great spiritual and cultural achievements, is a lost world and is incapable of saving itself and ordering its existence in a meaningful manner.

The process of secularization began when man exchanged the glory of the immortal God for the image of mortal man and the forms of the world of the created (Rom. 1:23). The process has continued during the course of the centuries, finally engulfing all aspects of human life—state and politics, society and individual, marriage and family, science and art, economy and technology. Secularization has withdrawn these areas far from the influence of the gospel and the commandments of God. The final stage of this process in regard to one's outlook on life and the world is nihilism. This nihilism is completely destructive and denies the validity of all religious and ethical values. It is that form of existentialism that, under the guise of humanism, proclaims the freedom of man by virtue of which man may form the world in his own manner. This freedom is completely atheistic since it rejects every commitment to God as well as the commandment of God demanding obedience.

Thus, it is the judgment of the New Testament that the world is evil (1 John 5:19). It lies under the power of the evil one and the time in which we live is the present evil age (Gal. 1:4). Men, as sons of this age (Luke 16:8), are of a dishonest generation (Acts 2:40; Phil. 2:15). Their works are fundamentally bad. They, despite their natural vitality and activity, are "dead through the trespasses and sins . . ., following the course of this world, following the prince of the power of the air, the spirit that is now at work in the sons of disobedience" (Eph. 2:1-3); "they are darkened in their

understanding, alienated from the life of God . . . , callous and have
given themselves up to licentiousness, greedy to practice every kind
of uncleanness" (Eph. 4:18-22). They are, therefore, by nature
"children of divine wrath" (Eph. 2:3).

Men live their lives as slaves of sin (Rom. 6:16) in the service of
human passions (1 Peter 4:2). Their actions and deeds are characterized by worldly passions (Titus 2:12) and sinful passions that come
from the lust of the eyes, the lust of the flesh, and the pride of life
(1 John 2:16; cf. Eph. 2:4). They give their members as weapons to the
service of sin (Rom. 6:15). The corruption of the world is due to this
way of being (2 Peter 1:4).

The world diminishes because of its lust (1 John 2:17), as it is
under the condemnation of God (Rom. 5:18). It will one day be
judged in the final judgment (1 Cor. 11:32).

THE WORLD UNDER THE MERCY OF GOD

The sinful world, which persists in its opposition to God, is the
same world that is subject to the words and deeds of God's revelation. As it exists under the wrath and the judgment of God, so it also
lives under his grace. Thus, there exists a history of salvation in the
midst of a history of doom. The history of salvation was first linked
to God's action with respect to the chosen people of Israel. Later,
however, with the appearance of Jesus Christ on earth, it encom-
passed all humankind. The life of Christ—the incarnation, the death
on the cross, and the resurrection of Christ—is the central event in
the history of salvation. His return in power and glory will be its
consummation.

With Christ, the turning point of time has come. God sent his
son into the *world,* so that the *world* may be saved through him
(John 3:17; 12:47). He so loved the *world* "that he gave his only son,
that whoever believes in him should not perish but have eternal
life" (John 3:16). In Christ, God reconciled the *world* to himself and
established the word of reconciliation (2 Cor. 5:19). God's decree of
salvation for the reconciliation of the *world* was attested at the cross
of Golgotha as the basic historical event of salvation. According to
Col. 1:19-20, this event has a cosmic significance that transcends

humanity and embraces the entire universe. It was the will of God, through Christ, to "reconcile to himself all things, whether on earth or in heaven."

Christ is the light of the *world* (John 8:12; 9:5), the bread of life which gives life to the *world* (John 6:33), the lamb of God who takes away the sin of the *world* (John 1:29). As the exalted one, he possesses all power in heaven and on earth (Matth. 28:18). As the heavenly Kyrios, he has been given a name which is above every name (Phil. 2:9). He is the head of all rule and authority (Col. 2:10).

THE RENEWED WORLD

With the end of this age, the rule of the powers of evil ends once and for all. The second coming of Christ leads to the full reestablishment of the rule of God in the total sphere of the cosmos. With the victory of Christ over the powers that oppose God, the dominion of the worldly and the superworldly powers is abolished. God's decree, the realization of which he has undertaken, is then achieved when that stage of development ordained by him has been reached: in Christ, as the head, "to unite all things in him, things in heaven and things on earth" (Eph. 1:10). Then the time will be when before him "every knee should bow, in heaven and on earth and under the earth and every tongue confess that Jesus Christ is Lord" (Phil. 2:10-11). Christ is the savior of the world, the Lord of the world, and the consummator of the world. At the end of all things stands a new heaven and a new earth. The world then belongs fully and wholly to God and his anointed one.

In our survey, we are concerned with a world that is determined by its apostasy from God, but which now, through Christ, stands under the sign of reconciliation. This marks the special position of the church toward the world. On the one hand, the church is turned away from the world and on the other hand, it is turned toward it. It is at the same time closed to the world and open to it. It is separated from the world and yet it has a task for the world.

Having thus briefly characterized the nature of the world on the basis of evidence found in the New Testament, we must now, in like manner, briefly define *the essence of the church.* We can summarize what the New Testament says about the church in four basic statements.

THE CHURCH IS THE ECCLESIA OF GOD, SAVED FROM THE WORLD AND THE PRESENT AGE

It is the people of God, devoted to God and sanctified by him, who confess Jesus Christ as head and lord of the church. The church comprises the people of God—redeemed, delivered by the blood of Christ, atoned—who by the forgiveness of sins stand in a state of salvation and grace. The church is no longer under the power of the prince of this age and the satanic-demonic powers, for it is now the uniting of the redeemed people of the new covenant, believing in Christ, justified, baptized in his name, and filled with the Holy Spirit. It is made up of the holy, who are chosen, called, and loved by God, who are resolved to do the will of God. Thus, it is the true Israel, the Israel of the spirit—"a chosen race, a royal priesthood, a holy nation, God's own people" (1 Peter 2:9).

THE CHURCH IS THE BEGINNING OF GOD'S NEW CREATION

This is true because it is the *church in Christ.* The members of the church have died with Christ, are made alive with him to a new life, and are raised up with him in the heavenly places (Eph. 2:5-6). Thus, the church has its basic existence in the realm of life and salvation of the exalted and living Christ. It is already removed from the world and its true life is hidden with Christ in God (Col. 3:3).

As the church of Christ, it is the *body of Christ,* and Christ as its head fulfills and permeates it with his spirit, his power, his life, and his love. Through the members of his body, Christ is active in the world. As the organ of Christ, characterized and marked by his being, the church can be compared to no other structure on earth. It is an organ of the spirit, formed by the gift of the spirit which has been given to it.

The Johannine concept of the church is marked by very characteristic statements, directed with special clarity toward the opposition of world and church. As men born anew, those believing in

Christ have a new origin. They are born of God (John 1:13; 1 John 4:5). In this way, their origin is lifted out of a world that opposes God and the consequences of such a world are removed. Thus, disciples of Jesus are no longer of the world because Jesus is no longer of the world (John 17:16). In the farewell speeches of the Gospel of John, Jesus said expressly to his disciples, "You are not of the world" (John 15:19). The reason for this is that Jesus elects his own people from the world, i.e., he has singled them out. From this follows quite logically the statement, "For whatever is born of God overcomes the world; and this is the victory that overcomes the world, our faith" (1 John 5:4).

THE CHURCH IS UNDER THE
RULING POWER OF THE EXALTED CHRIST

Christ has assumed the heavenly throne (Col. 3:1). He is seated at the right hand of the Majesty on high (Heb. 1:3), from where he exercises his power. He rules as king and the church is the holy people which bows to his claim of lordship and knows that it is bound to him for service and obedience. It is the instrument for the execution of his will on earth. Christ's claim to lordship excludes all human autonomy, for Christians must no longer live for themselves but for Christ who, for their sake, died and was raised (2 Cor. 5:15). Within the saving deed of Christ lies the deepest ground for the ministry of the church. It is a ministry of the spirit and of love, of devotion to Christ and to the brethren, a service to the honor of God and to the salvation of the world.

The obedience rendered by the church to its Lord is a joyous obedience, for Christ the Lord loves the church. The purpose of his lordship is to present the church "in glorious splendor," that it might be holy and without blemish (Eph. 5:27). Thus, the lordship of Christ is directed toward the perfection of the church and, in the end, toward the submission of the whole cosmos.

The church, which is subjugated to the lordship of Christ, waits for the second advent of Christ at which time he will be revealed in all his power and glory to the whole world. Then the church, which through resurrection from the dead will be likened to his glorious body (Phil. 3:21), will rule with him in all eternity.

THE CHURCH, WHICH IS THE CHURCH IN CHRIST, IS AT THE SAME TIME THE CHURCH IN THE WORLD

Christians are at once separated from the world as such, but find themselves bound to the world by their earthly bodies. They stand in the orders of this world, although in their essence they already belong to the order of the new aeon. Their existence in the world gives rise to the temptation and peril of the church, which lives in continuous tension with the world.

Hence, the church has a highly paradoxical existence. It is characterized by the "already" and the "not yet," redeemed from the world yet placed in its midst. It lives in the time of salvation begun with the event of Christ and yet the time of evil has not yet come to an end. It is the church of the end of time, and still, it is not yet the church of the eschatological consummation.

Thus, we arrive at our second thesis.

CHAPTER TWO

Church and World Relate to Each Other

THE INFLUENCE OF THE CHURCH ON THE WORLD

THE DISCIPLES OF Jesus are sent into the world just as Jesus was sent into the world by God (John 17:18). Consequently Jesus, in a high-priestly prayer (John 17:15), asks not that God take the disciples out of the world, but that he keep them from the evil one in the world.

The church of Jesus is the salt of the earth (Matth. 5:13) and the light of the world (Matth. 5:14). It has the task of penetrating the world with the saving power of the gospel of divine grace and love. The commission of the risen Christ, "Go into all the world and preach the gospel to the whole creation" (Mark 16:15), is of fundamental importance and commanding authority for the church. The universal commission of Jesus, in the final words of the risen Christ as reported by Matthew, has an even more definite form: "Make disciples of all nations, baptizing them in the name of the Father and of the Son and of the Holy Spirit, teaching them to observe all that I have commanded you." In the interpretation of the parable of

the weeds among the wheat, Jesus said that the field on which the
Son of Man sows the good seed is the world (Matth. 13:38). And
when Paul, the greatest apostle of Jesus Christ, made the world, as it
was then known, to be the object of the mission, he was fulfilling the
demand of the divine Master with ardent zeal and undivided commitment. Thus, Paul is able to confess in Col. 1:23 that the gospel
"has been preached to every creature, and . . . I, Paul, became (its)
minister."

The church, in carrying out its missionary service, must fulfill a
threefold task:

First, it must witness to the world the gospel of Jesus Christ
and, to the complete exclusion of all other cults of salvation to proclaim that "there is salvation in no one else, for there is no other
name under heaven given among men by which we must be saved"
(Acts 4:12). It makes the absolute claim that Jesus Christ is *the*
Savior of the world and *the* Lord over all powers and authorities,
over all thrones and dominions and that the way to God, to the forgiveness of sins, and to eternal salvation is exclusively through faith
in Jesus Christ. Its basic task consists of winning men to Christ
by proclaiming the word and building the church of Christ through
the power of the Holy Spirit.

*Second, the church has the task of allowing the healing powers
of Christ to become active in the world.* The church is given the gifts
of the Spirit and by this power, it can do mighty deeds, miracles, and
healing of diseases and it can do the works of love. It has its own
dynamic characteristic, which is not only related to the world but
also to the power of the signs that accompany the proclamation.

*Third, the church has the task of overcoming the demonic
powers.* It is given the authority to penetrate the sphere of the
enemy of God and to destroy the strongholds of Satan (2 Cor. 10:4).
The word of God entrusted to the church has the power to penetrate
the deepest abysses of the human soul and to deliver men from the
nefarious bonds that destroy life, to rid them of their enslavement to
passion and lust and restore the order ordained by God in their
intellectual, spiritual, and bodily existence. The ministry of spiritual

care encompasses the whole man who is subjected to powers hostile to God.

In this way, the church has the task of continuing, through the Holy Spirit, the whole work of Christ on earth. For it is the instrument with which Christ establishes his lordship in the world.

But the movement of the church *toward the world* corresponds to the movement coming from the world and directed *against the church.*

THE INFLUENCE OF THE WORLD ON THE CHURCH

The godless world sees as its task the breaking of the power of Christ as revealed in the church. As it has dethroned God, crucified Christ, and set up its idols in place of God's glory, it rejects the gospel of salvation and works for the destruction of the church in order that the world may march united under the lordship of the prince of this age. The world which God loves rejects his love and is in a constant state of rebellion against God. It does not heed the disciples of Jesus, but rather the false prophets who speak of the world (1 John 4:5). Thus, it hates the disciples of Jesus just as it hated Jesus (John 17:14). The world is alien toward the church and views it as a foreign element. Consequently, its efforts are directed towards hindering the church in carrying out its duty, using the coercive means at its disposal in covert or overt battle, not stopping short of bloody persecution. Its ultimate goal is the destruction of the church.

The world, which does the will of the prince of this age, not only works from without against the church, it avails itself of subtler and more refined means to paralyze the church from within. It undermines the church, sapping its substance by questioning the truth of its doctrine, weakening the strength of its faith, and threatening its vital moral power. In a word, it endeavors to bring the "world" into the church and destroy its holy nature. The ultimate goal is the inner weakening of the church, i.e., its secularization. The church that has become like the world is the end of the church of Christ.

Satan sows the seed of doubt and disbelief in the hearts of believers. He makes them unsure of their insight and prevents them from arriving at a clear decision for Christ. Satan wants to snatch away the word that is sowed in the heart of man (Matth. 13:19), or at least to restate the age-old question, "Did God really say this?"

Conformity to the world is the great inner danger for the church, for then the desire for sanctification and the longing to be molded in the image of Christ cease. The secularized church is no longer involved in the glorification of Christ and the praise of God.

The same objective is reached when the church loses the power of critical judgment and allows the infusion of perceptions of life and the world that are contrary to the revelation of God in Jesus Christ. In the time of primitive Christianity, Judaism, libertinism, and gnosticism were such foes. Today world views are the foes which have severed all connections with the biblical basis of faith, whether they be called idealism, materialism, nihilism, or some other name.

The greatest danger comes from heresies that purport to proclaim Christian truths, but actually shift the doctrine off-center. They claim to mediate more profound insights, but they actually falsify the revealed truth by diluting the word of God with human wisdom or demythologize it to such a degree as to render the power of the gospel ineffectual. Heresy always threatens the substance of true doctrine and attacks its foundations. The heretics, as Paul describes them in 2 Cor. 11:13-14, are "false apostles, deceitful workmen, disguising themselves as apostles of Christ. And no wonder, for even Satan disguises himself as an angel of light." Therefore, the church is exhorted, "Do not believe every spirit, but test the spirits to see whether they are of God; for many false prophets have gone out into the world" (1 John 4:1).

The church's inner essence is also threatened when the divine commandments and orders are disregarded and moral life is subjugated to the norms of the world. This threat is stronger today than previously because life confronts us today with many unanswered questions. And it is a task which cannot be taken seriously enough in Christian ethics to give clear, unequivocal answers to these questions. Here, much pastoral wisdom is needed and the decisions that must be made in individual concrete cases are often very difficult.

But in no case should they be contrary to the spirit of the gospel, but rather they must conform with the moral demands of Jesus and the apostles. Today more than ever the enemy of the church seeks to activate the flesh against the spirit so that Christians are no longer men of the spirit, but men who fall prey to the temptations of the flesh, the lusts, and the passions.

The world's main points of attack are the falsification of the gospel and the erosion of moral principles.

Thus, the relationship between church and world is marked by a state of struggle. The church has the task of influencing the world and winning it for Christ, but from the world comes constant threat and temptation directed toward the church.

The church can endure this struggle only because it has a Lord who is more powerful than the world. It has the promise that not even the power of death shall prevail against it (Matth. 16:18). To it were made the promises of Jesus, "I am with you always, to the close of the age" (Matth. 28:20) and "I give them eternal life, and they shall never perish, and no one shall snatch them out of my hand. My Father, who has given them to me, is greater than all, and no one is able to snatch them out of the Father's hand" (John 10:28-29). And finally, "In the world you have tribulation; but be of good cheer, I have overcome the world" (John 16:33).

Jesus has overcome the world. Thus, the church can be full of confidence. "For the form of this world passes away, and the lust of it; but he who does the will of God abides for ever" (1 John 2:17).

The power of the church lies within the living faith in the living Lord. "For whatever is born of God overcomes the world; and this is the victory that overcomes the world, our faith" (1 John 5:4).

CHAPTER THREE

The Church and the Secular Orders of Life

WE HAVE ALREADY touched lightly on this point but now we must examine it in greater detail for here we are dealing with actualities that affect the relationship between the church and the world in a very concrete manner.

The church, by its eschatological determination, belongs already to the coming age. In its deepest essence it is a new creation in Christ, and is, therefore, subject to the orders of the kingdom of God. However, the church is at the same time a church in the world, thus being subject to the orders of this age. It follows that the church is in a state of tension between the orders of this world and the future orders, which are already active and lay claim to the church.

We must clarify its significance in relation to individual aspects of life by applying evidence found in the New Testament.

THE POSITION OF THE CHURCH WITH RESPECT TO THE STATE

The New Testament contains no political theories nor do we find any statements giving preference to any certain form of government or which develop a new revolutionary idea of the state. Rather, the state is accepted as it is. Undoubtedly, this is due to the eschatological expectation dominating Jesus and primitive Christianity. A new order of all things comes with the establishment of the Kingdom of God, which signifies the end of all earthly states.

Jesus made a clear distinction between the kingdom of the world and that of God. This is the meaning of the statement, "Render to Caesar the things that are Caesar's, and to God the things that are God's" (Mark 12:17). Jesus recognized the power of the state, approved its rightful claims, and committed his disciples to obedience to the state's demands (Matth. 17:24-27) as long as these demands did not exceed their proper authority. If the state respects the demands of God, then its authority is unimpeachable. If, however, it interferes in the course of the redemptive process, as in the case of Jesus, it sins against God, even though—and this is the mystery of divine salvation—by its death sentence against Jesus, it serves in the realization of the divine plan of salvation. Jesus also left no doubt in the minds of his disciples that when the state exceeds its given limits, they must suffer persecution (Mark 13:9-13), being brought before the courts to answer to governors and kings. These persecutions, which may possibly lead to martyrdom, serve, in the final analysis, in the building of the church according to God's mysterious plan of salvation.

Further, Jesus did not hesitate to pay the temple tax (Matth. 17:24). To the question of the Roman state's right to collect tolls and taxes from the Jewish people Jesus answered, to be sure, that in theory it did not, but still he suggested that his disciples pay the required taxes, in order "not to give offense to them" (Matth. 17:27).

However, Jesus made a statement that is too often neglected in which he characterized *the essence of the state.* Mark 10:42 reads, "You know that those who are supposed to rule over the Gentiles lord it over them, and their great men exercise authority over them." This statement shows that Jesus had deep insight into the state's methods of exercising power. That he did not approve of these methods is clear from his instructions to the disciples: "But it shall not be so among you . . . but whoever would be first among you must be servant of all" (Mark 10:43-44). Thus, Jesus drew two lines of demarcation: (1) between the kingdom of the earth and that of God, and (2) between the power of the state and the discipleship. He recognized the right of the state, if it fulfills its task in its own proper realm without exceeding its given powers. From his disciples, however, he demanded conduct in their lives that stood in contrast to the state's exercise of power. Within the congregation of the disciples, a new order built on the idea of service which knows no compulsion and no hierarchy is realized.

Finally, all this is within the framework of *the eschatological proviso*, which rests on apocalyptic traditions: the state has meaning only within this age. When the Kingdom of God on Earth has been established, the kingdom of this world will have come to an end.

In Romans 13, Paul made the basic statement concerning his view of the state. God instituted the state. Accordingly, it is everyone's duty to subject himself to those in power. He who opposes them is rebelling against the order of God. When the authorities punish the evil doers or even impose the death penalty, they are acting as the servants of God. Thus, in the authorities, Paul sees the executive organ of divine justice to which the Christian subjects himself not out of fear, but from the free responsibility of his conscience (Romans 13:5). For this reason he also pays the revenues, taxes, and customs due the state. He knows that the officers of the state are "ministers of God" (Romans 13:6).

When Paul speaks of the state, he is describing *the essential structure of a state of law* acting in moral responsibility and whose authority is anchored in God. The problem of the degenerated state that misuses its power and terrorizes its subjects is not taken up by Paul in Romans 13. He has in mind the well ordered state of the Roman Empire in which he enjoys the rights of citizenship and in which there has not yet been a serious conflict with the church of Christ.

Subordination to the power of the authorities is also demanded in Titus 3:1 and 1 Peter 2:13-14. It is expressly emphasized in 1 Peter 2:13 that obedience to the king (emperor) or the governors shall be given "for the Lord's sake." In addition to due obedience comes intercession on behalf of the state (1 Tim. 2:1-2).

But Paul, too, recognizes *the eschatological proviso.* At the end of time, the secular states and powers of the world are replaced by the Kingdom of Christ and finally by the Kingdom of God. In 1 Cor. 15:24 Paul declares, "Then comes the end, when he delivers the kingdom to God the Father after destroying every rule and every authority and power. For he must reign until he has put all his enemies under his feet."

But in addition, we find in Paul the insight that Christ has already assumed his lordship as the exalted over both the church and the world. The rule of Christ is already a reality, even though according to the nature of this age the prince of this world (Satan) still exercises his power. The unrestricted rule of Christ will be revealed only at his second coming.

With the realization that Christ, by his exaltation to the throne of God's glory, has already assumed his rule of the world, it follows that Christians, regardless of their membership in the secular state, are citizens of the heavenly *polis,* the city of God. They have their citizenship in heaven (Phil. 3:21). Thus, they are citizens of two forms of state, one secular and one heavenly. Accordingly they have a double responsibility: on the one hand to the ruling power of the state and on the other hand to Christ's claim of lordship. It is obvious that this situation involves a serious problem.

If the state disregards the heavenly citizenship of Christians with the consequential handicapping of the church's actions and if it exceeds the powers ordained for it by God, what then must be done?

The first answer to this question is given in Acts 5:6: in case of conflict, one must obey God more than men (cf. also Acts 4:19). The second answer, more significant for the history of the church, is found in Rev. 13. The state that idolizes itself and, in its emperor cult, demands the veneration of the dragon and the beast from the abyss, blasphemes God and subjects his saints to religious terror, drives the Christians to disobedience and resistance. Yet, despite all this, the basic loyalty of Christians toward the state remains intact, although Christians oppose with an absolute "no" those measures of the state that represent a transgression of its proper authority and lead to complete disregard of divine right.

It follows that the relationship of the Christian to the state is not to be defined on the basis of Romans 13 alone. In case of conflict, subordination of the Christian to the lordship of God and Christ is preferred to subordination to the state. Christ is then the sole emperor, not Caesar.

THE POSITION WITH RESPECT TO MARRIAGE

Here again things are not as simple as perceived by the secular sphere. For both Jesus and the apostles, marriage is a divine creation, but this is not all there is to say on the subject.

Jesus demanded the insolubility of marriage and intensified the prohibition of adultery by condemning not only the accomplished act, but even the lustful look at the wife of one's neighbor. Marriage is insoluble because in marriage husband and wife "are no longer two but one flesh" (Mark 10:8). For this reason Jesus rejects the right of a husband—given in the Mosaic law (Deut. 24:1)—to give his wife a bill of divorce and dismiss her. What was valid from the beginning of creation—"What therefore God has joined together, let no man put asunder"—is of absolute validity for the disciples. In Mark 10:11-12, Jesus states specifically, "Whoever divorces his wife and marries another, commits adultery against her; and if she divorces her husband and marries another, she commits adultery" (cf. Matth. 5:32).

Here too, however, *the eschatological proviso* is valid. Marriage is an institution of this age: "For in the resurrection they neither marry nor are given in marriage, but are like angels in heaven" (Matth. 22:30).

Beyond this, in words more suggestive than clearly expressed, Jesus envisaged an order of life within this age that implies an anticipation of the eschatological order. In Matthew 19:12 he speaks of those who are unfit for marriage, who have become unfit for the sake of the Kingdom of Heaven. However we interpret in detail the words of Jesus, "He who is able to receive this, let him receive it," it is nonetheless clear that Jesus approved sexual asceticism, even though he did not demand it. Asceticism was a matter of course for him, although in other instances he did not deny himself the simple pleasures of life as seen in Matthew 11:19. Complete devotion to the Kingdom of God could lead to the renunciation of marriage and family, and Matthew 19:12 shows that Jesus was not alone in this attitude. However, Jesus never said that the unmarried status should be placed above the married status. Yet, Matthew 19:12 indicates that, even during the time of Jesus, renunciation of marriage was a reality within the narrower or wider circle of disciples.

Paul went a step beyond Jesus. Paul fully affirmed matrimony. Dissolution of a Christian marriage is out of the question for Paul as it also was for Jesus. Even in cases of mixed marriages between Christians and heathens, he demanded that the request for separation in such a marriage never come from the Christian partner (1 Cor. 7:12-13). For Paul, the latter is duty-bound by Christ's command to maintain the marriage and the mixed marriage is sanctified by the Christian husband or the Christian wife. Things are different if the unbelieving partner in marriage presses for divorce. In this case, "the brother or sister" is not bound to the marriage like a slave (1 Cor. 7:15).

Paul is also of the opinion that, where it exists, marriage should be consummated in the full sense of marital relations. The apostle allows an exception only for times of especially intensive religious practice (1 Cor. 7:5), but such an arrangement should be made only by mutual agreement.

Yet, according to the personal judgment of Paul, the unmarried life is to be preferred to the married: "I wish that all were as I myself am (namely unmarried)" (1 Cor. 7:7). Paul then explains that each has his own special gift, one of one kind (unmarried) and one of another (married). It is far from Paul's wish to demand too much of the Christian husband or the Christian wife. He concedes to everyone, not only according to his own natural predisposition, but especially according to his God-given charisma, the freedom of choice. However, Paul makes one important argument in favor of unmarried life. The single person can concentrate more on religious tasks because he is not diverted from spiritual things by earthly cares. He "is anxious about the affairs of the Lord, how to please the Lord; but the married man is anxious about worldly affairs, how to please his wife, and his interests are divided. And the unmarried woman or girl is anxious about the affairs of the Lord, how to be holy in body and spirit, but the married woman or girl is anxious about the [affairs of this world, how to please her husband]" (1 Cor. 7:32-34). But here an idea is revealed that will be of great importance and that has a strong bearing on our present topic: the married Christian is bound more closely to the world than the unmarried Christian. The unmarried Christian is farther removed from the world. This is a decisive point for Paul. Another point is that the unmarried Christian, since he can devote more of his life to the Lord, has a greater opportunity to become a spiritual man. Unlike the married Christian, he is not constantly drawn into the sphere of the flesh. Thus, it is only partly correct to attribute Paul's preference of the unmarried status to his eschatological expectation alone. Certainly, the conviction that the end of the age was at hand plays an important role in his thought (1 Cor. 7:29), but the reasons stated above are decisive. The purely eschatological aspect is that life without marriage is anticipation of the order of the coming age. Thus, our assertion is confirmed here as well that the order of creation is indeed a divine order of life, but that the order of the future age transcends it. This order is already being realized by those who have the charisma of celibacy.

The pastoral wisdom of Paul in the question of marriage or no marriage is most clearly expressed in 1 Cor. 7:26-28: "I think that in view of the present distress it is well for a person to remain as he is (unmarried). Are you bound to a wife? Do not seek to be free. Are you free from a wife? Do not seek marriage. But if you marry, you do not sin, and if a girl marries she does not sin. Yet those who marry will have worldly troubles, and I would spare you that."

The same concept determines Paul's advice concerning *the remarriage of widows* (1 Cor. 7:39-40). The Christian widow is free to marry whomever she wishes. The apostle sets only one limitation: it should take place "in the Lord," i.e., the widow should not marry a heathen.

A mixed marriage is justified only where the marriage existed before one of the partners came to believe. But in a case where the woman has the opportunity to marry a second time, after the death of her husband, she must be careful to see that the man believes in Christ and belongs to the church. The marriage should be contracted within the life and under the lordship of Christ and exist in him. This is the order that is valid for the church. And yet, here too Paul goes a step further. He explains: the widow is to be considered happier if she remains unmarried. To be sure, Paul specifically emphasizes that this is his personal opinion. Still, he adds emphasis and weight to his opinion by appealing to the authority of the spirit: "I think that I have the spirit of God." Thus, he brings to bear the spiritual power of his apostolic authority without falling into legalism. Whereas he cannot claim an expressed command of the Lord, he refers to the guidance of the spirit. Yet, where the spirit of the Lord is, there is freedom even in questions of personal conscience and way of life.

In his letter to Timothy, Paul's judgment is sharper regarding *younger widows of marriageable age* (1 Timothy 5:11-15). Here the counsel is given that these widows, when they are unable to endure enforced celibacy, should remarry, become mothers, preside over their household, "and give the enemy no reason to revile us" (1 Timothy 5:14). But this measure, necessary for practical reasons, is somewhat limited through the pronouncement that widows who remarry "incur condemnation for having violated their first pledge" (1 Timothy 5:12). The thought behind Paul's statements in 1 Cor. 7 that widows would be better off not marrying is absent in his first letter to Timothy. It is only faintly reflected in 1 Timothy 5:11 where he states that the really normal behavior of widows should be devotion to Christ. If devotion to Christ is not sufficiently strong to overcome her "sensual excitement," then remarriage is recommended. This whole argumentation issues from a well thought out pastoral insight, but it does not have the spiritual stature of 1 Cor. 7:39-40 and Romans 7:2-3, where Paul allows widows their full freedom of decision and where remarriage is not branded as disloyalty to the deceased husband, as is the case in 1 Timothy 5:12.

A *widow who is completely alone and does not consider remarriage* fulfills her widowhood in the proper way, according to 1 Timothy 5:5, when she "has set her hope on God and continues in supplications and prayers night and day." Her primary task is the intensive life of prayer.

A frequently discussed question is how the counsel of the apostle in 1 Cor. 7:36-38, directed toward unmarried girls, is to be understood. In any case, it is difficult to deduct from the text whether it is referring to a spiritual betrothal, i.e., a relationship between a single man and a single woman (*virgines introductae*) that resembles marriage but is completely ascetic, or whether it should be interpreted as Paul discussing the question of how a father should react if his daughter, who has passed the "years of her youth," is in a hurry to marry.

The latter explanation is probably the correct one, although it does not answer all the questions involved in the text. If we follow this explanation, then we obtain the following instruction from Paul that corresponds completely to the apostle's basic principle concerning marriage and celibacy. Paul says: the father is free in his decision. If, under the given circumstances, he gives his daughter permission to marry, he does not sin. If, however, he is not being pressured by his daughter, i.e., if she does not absolutely insist on being married, then he is justified in his decision to leave his virgin daughter unmarried. But here, too, Paul's true opinion appears in the sentence that is typical of his entire discussion of the marriage question: "He who marries his betrothed does well; and he who refrains from marriage will do better" (1 Cor. 7:38).

For Paul, as for all primitive Christianity, all *extramarital sexual relations* are out of the question. Unchastity has nothing to do with Christian freedom. For the Christian, it is unthinkable licentiousness of fleshly lust. Thus, unchastity is not a sign of true freedom because, in intercourse with a whore, the man enters a relationship that is sinful and contrary to divine commandment. For "he who joins himself to a prostitute becomes one body with her" (1 Cor. 6:16). The apostle rejects extramarital sexual relations with a prostitute on very serious religious grounds. Here he is in sharp contrast to Greek thinking which held that a prostitute in the service of the god was a hierodule who offered herself as part of the temple cult and whose ways and doings were considered a part of worship. In contrast to this, Paul says that the body of the Christian exists for the Lord. It is a temple of the Holy Spirit which, in contrast to the pagan temple, must be free of all unchastity, for unchastity and the Holy Spirit are separated from each other by an abyss that cannot be bridged. Paul also justifies the purity of the Christian's body with a reference to the body of Christ. The Christian's members are the members of Christ (1 Cor. 6:15). Through sexual relations of a Christian with a heathen prostitute, since in sexual relations two bodies become one, the grotesque and completely preposterous situation would arise where the members that belong to Christ become the members of a prostitute. In the final analysis, it would be the unification of the body of Christ with the body of the heathen prostitute, but this would be a blasphemy beyond comparison. Christians have the task of honoring God with their body. He who belongs to Christ becomes one spirit with him. Thus, the profound union with Christ and the belonging to the body of Christ that is based on this union completely excludes the physical union of the Christian with the prostitute, even if she is acting as a hierodule. For the pagan temple cult, in any form, is idolatry and not the worship of God. The theoretical possibility that the physical union of Christians in extramarital sexual relations might not be considered unchastity because it involves two bodies dedicated to Christ is not even considered by Paul because this would be in stark contradiction to the order of the creator, according to which man and woman can become one flesh only in marriage.

With all this, of course, one question remains: do we find in Paul a full understanding of Christian marriage? With all the arguments made by the apostle in favor of celibacy, we must answer by saying that he does not do full justice to the deep values found in a true Christian marriage and that Paul does not fully appreciate the blessing that comes from such a marriage to the partners themselves, to the family, and to all those whom they serve together in their responsibility before God.

An *echo of the Pauline evaluation of celibacy* is found in the Revelation to John. In the vision of the perfect church of 144,000 on Mount Zion, those are praised "who have not defiled themselves with women, for they are chaste" (Rev. 14:4). It should not be overlooked that in Revelation the church is called the bride of the lamb (Rev. 22:17) and that in 2 Cor. 11:2 Paul has spoken of the church as a pure bride, whom he has betrothed to one man, Christ, in order to lead her to him. When the marriage of the Lamb is spoken of (Rev. 19:7-9), it depicts a picture of the complete union of the church with Christ. The marriage itself, however, is purely spiritual in nature in accordance with the essence of the new age. At this time a completely new order with respect to marriage will appear, having only the name in common with the institution of this age. This is also the case in Eph. 5:32 where the apostle parallels the "profound mystery" in the unity of man and wife in earthly marriage with the relationship of Christ to the church.

THE PRINCIPLE OF SUPERIORITY AND INFERIORITY

The secular orders of life, according to Paul's teaching, are determined by the principle of superiority and inferiority. Only in this way, in the judgment of the apostle, can there be a meaningful state and meaningful marriage.

In marriage the wife is subjugated to the husband (1 Cor. 11:3; 1 Peter 3:1; Titus 2:5). This follows from the order of creation, according to which the man is the image and glory of God, while the woman is the glory of the man (1 Cor. 11:7). God assigned woman the subordinate position by first creating man and then woman. "For man was not made from woman, but woman from man" (1 Cor. 11:8-9).

But this fact of creation must not lead to the disdain of women. "In the Lord," i.e., in the realm of the life and lordship of Christ, "woman is not independent of man nor man of woman" (1 Cor. 11:11). Since the partners in marriage are one in the Lord, they form a homogenous whole. In Christ they *belong to each other.* Thus, Paul makes a distinction between the realm of creation and that of

Christ. In the realm of creation, woman is subordinate to man. In the realm of Christ, they are equal.

But even the natural order of life indicates the value of woman, as given her by the creation, and the dignity that comes from this. For the statement that woman has her origin in man must be complemented by the fact that man is born of woman. Thus, woman is an important member of the creation process, which is ordained by God and occurs ever anew in human birth.

Even if woman has been subordinate to man since the beginning of creation, it does not mean that in the Christian marriage the husband has autonomous sovereignty or even high-handed, dictatorial power. His superior position with respect to his wife is secure from all arbitrariness and extremes since he himself is subject to a superior: Christ. Thus, Paul explains in 1 Cor. 11:3, "The head of every man is Christ, the head of a woman is her husband, and the head of Christ is God." It is this order that includes Christ and God which gives the prevailing order in marriage its deepest meaning and its ultimate responsibility.

In the letter to the Ephesians (5:24), the proper relationship of man and woman in marriage is compared to the order within the church: "As the church is subject to Christ, so let wives also be subject in everything to their husbands." Since Christ, as head, has loved the church and given himself for it, it follows that the husband cannot act as a strict master over his wife. Rather, he is to love and cherish her, and the wife should have respect for her husband. If these principles are followed, then a healthy, stable, and truly Christian married life is guaranteed.

There is also agreement in fulfilling the duties of marriage. In tender words, Paul demands mutual regard, which eliminates the possibility of excess demands on the part of the husband or the wife. He formulates this in 1 Cor. 7:3-4 in the following manner: "The husband should give to his wife her conjugal rights, and likewise the wife to her husband. For the wife does not rule over her own body, but the husband does; likewise the husband does not rule over his own body, but the wife does. In the Christian marriage, neither the husband nor the wife is abandoned to the inconsiderate, egotistic sexual demands of the other partner. The rights of the husband should not render the wife without rights, and the claims of the wife must not make the husband a tool of the wife, without a will of his own. Neither the husband nor the wife may fall prey to extreme lust and instinctive passion; otherwise the spiritual substance of Christian marriage is gravely endangered and its deepest mystery in the Lord is threatened."

Likewise, First Thessalonians admonishes husbands to hold their wives in "holiness and honor" and not in the passion of lust, as the heathen who do not know God. The First Letter of Peter (3:7) demands that husbands live together with their wives in a reasonable manner, bestowing the honor that is due them. If husbands do not do this, it will have a disastrous effect on the spiritual life of the partners, "in order that your prayers not be hindered." If in 1 Cor. 7:5 Paul has indicated that for partners in marriage there can be times of especially intense prayer, then it follows that the Christian marriage, in which man and wife are bound to Christ, has its deepest foundation in common prayer and that the nurturing of the spiritual life is one of the most important tasks of the Christian marriage.

An important task of the Christian wife with respect to her non-believing husband is derived from the principle that wives should be subjugated to their husbands. The Christian wife should assume and affirm the proper position given her by way of the order of creation so that her husband, through her moral behavior in the fear of God, may be won to Christ even without the use of words. Thus, the Christian wife serves the order of salvation by submitting herself to the divinely inspired order of creation and, at the same time, she is an immense and impressive witness for Christ. Her most precious adornment is not the braiding of her hair, the decoration of gold, and the wearing of fine clothing, but the deep down hidden person, "with the imperishable jewel of a gentle and quiet spirit" (1 Peter 3:4).

But more than that, the wife as a member of the body of Christ is equal in all respects to the husband. In Christ, the order of the future age is already accomplished. Therefore, *in him* there is neither male nor female, but they are one in him (Gal. 3:28). For in

Christ, the differences in this world are removed. Thus, Paul recognizes an order of Christ that is superior to the order of creation. Of course, in the concrete, earthly church these orders still stand in tension to each other. The tension will be removed only when the second coming of Christ brings the time of salvation to completion. Even now the order of Christ reigns in the church to the extent that it gives the Christian wife the gift of grace and gives her the right to pray and prophesy at church meetings, i.e., to deliver spiritual addresses (1 Cor. 11:5). Most important, however, the wife is joint heir to the grace of life (1 Peter 3:7).

THE PARENT-CHILD RELATIONSHIP IN THE FAMILY

As the relationship of husband and wife in marriage is fundamentally regulated by the principle of superiority and inferiority, so is the relationship of parents and children in the family.

Children should be obedient to their parents. The order recognized by the world is justified spiritually because obedience should take place "in the Lord." Only this metaphysical anchoring makes the children's duty of obedience a task of the deepest Christian responsibility.

The relationship of *fathers* to their children is also determined by this same responsibility. Fathers must bring up their children in the discipline and instruction of the Lord (Eph. 6:4). They should raise happy children, devoted to the Lord, but they must not abuse their authority. There must not be any bitter, sulky, or intimidated children in a Christian family.

Over and above these normal relationships within the family, Jesus establishes the case in which confession of faith in him breaks the family's narrow bonds of blood so that for his sake the members of the family go separate ways. He told his disciples, "He who loves father or mother more than me is not worthy of me; and he who loves son or daughter more than me is not worthy of me" (Matth. 10:37; Luke 14:26). But when the natural order of the family, established in the creation, is broken for the sake of Christ, then a higher order of the Kingdom of God takes its place—the family of God. It can then be said that "whoever does the will of my father in heaven is my brother, and sister, and mother" (Matth. 12:50; cf. Mark 3:34-35, Luke 8:21—"Whoever does the will of God is my brother, and sister, and mother"). The human family is not despised, but it does not represent the highest value, which is the family of the children of God, founded by Jesus.

THE SOCIAL ORDER

The principle of superiority and inferiority also determines the social structure. Of course, the servant must obey his master in all things, but the Christian subordinate is in a different situation from the non-Christian. The Christian acts out of a deeper sense of responsibility than the latter because he serves his earthly master as a servant of Christ (Eph. 6:6). In Colossians 3:23, Paul commands, "Whatever your task, work heartily, as serving the Lord and not men."

The same thought is expressed in the First Letter of Peter, but here (1 Peter 2:18-25) the statements take on special significance by the reference to the suffering of Christ, which he bore with patience, becoming a model for all who suffer unjustly. When slaves, who are subject not only to kind and gentle masters, but also to capricious and cruel ones, are mistreated in spite of their good behavior, they must fulfill their duty to obedience nonetheless. If, under these conditions, the slave endures patiently, then he receives the grace of God.

Primitive Christianity had no thoughts of changing existing social conditions, neither by reform nor by revolution. Nor did it influence state authorities in any way in order to ease the lot of slaves or to improve their position. This was due, first of all, to the fact that the church, with its insignificant influence in public life, had no chance of doing this and secondly—and this was the decisive point—the position of the church and its leading figures was determined by the certainty that this world, with all its orders of life, is transient and that the return of Christ and the establishment of his lordship would bring about a completely new order.

In 1 Timothy 6:1-2 the duty of obedience is also seen from a higher point of view. Slaves should regard their masters with the proper honor so that the name of God and the Christian teachings may not be defamed. The faithful service of the Christian slave serves the glory of God and by the willing fulfillment of the duties given him, the Christian slave demonstrates that in him life and teaching are one. Thus, by his actions, he becomes a silent witness to the word of salvation.

A special problem rises from the *relationship between the Christian slave and the Christian master*. The understanding of common brotherhood can lead to the point where the slave "brother" no longer sees the master "brother" as the real master, the one to whom he is subject, and he does not pay him the necessary respect and under certain circumstances he even treats his master with disrespect. In this regard work relationships suffer and the basic principle of superiority and subordination is threatened. Work discipline as well as the labor process itself can at this point be impaired. Therefore the warning is given to the Christian slave in 1 Timothy 6:2 that they must serve all the better, since those who benefit by their service are believers and beloved who make a point of treating their slaves in a kindly manner. Thus, Christian brotherhood must not disrupt the necessary labor relationships and must not question the authority of the Christian master.

On the other hand, in Philemon, verse 16, Paul instructs the Christian master that the Christian slave is not to be seen just as a slave, but "more than a slave, as a beloved brother."

Like the Christian servant, *the Christian master* is responsible to Christ. The principle established by Paul in 1 Cor. 7:3-4 for marriage has analogous use here: the Christian master must know that he has a master above him in heaven to whom he is accountable (Col. 4:1; Eph. 6:9). Thus, the Christian social structure is metaphysically anchored, just as the family life is. In this respect it is different from the secular social order.

Paul expounds upon the slave question even further in 1 Cor. 7:21-22. According to his general principle that each person should remain in the state in which he was called (1 Cor. 7:20), the apostle tells the Christian slave, "Were you a slave when called? Never mind. But if you can gain your freedom, [make use of your present

condition instead]" (1 Cor. 7:21). The apostle gives a religious basis
for this rigorous demand: in Christ, the slave is free and in the
church there is no difference between slave and master. In 1 Cor.
7:22 Paul states it in this manner: "For he who was called in the Lord
as a slave is a freedman of the Lord. Likewise he who was free when
called is a slave of Christ." The slave is a freedman of the Lord in that
he has been redeemed from the slavery of sin and the forces of evil in
this world in the manner of the sacral antique redemption of slaves
by way of a ransom—the precious blood of Christ. The freedom
given him in this way is higher and more valuable than freedom
from the discretion of the earthly master. Through the order that
reigns in the church, the problem of slavery in the earthly realm is
not solved, to be sure, but it is solved on a higher plane, in the realm
of Christ. In the church, Christ gives the slave what the world is not
prepared to give him: his freedom. For in Christ and in the church,
the eschatologically determined order of life of the new age is
already realized. It stands high above all earthly social orders which,
in relation to it, have only relative value and thus for the Christian are
no longer of significant meaning. Or stated differently, that which
was not obtainable in the earthly realm during the days of the
original Christians is already realized in the realm of Christ and of
the church. The church is the place where the order of the coming
age, the just social order, is presented in advance. The slave is a full
member of the church, a brother in Christ, like every other member.

Finally, Paul comes to the recognition that *in Christ* all orders
of the earthly realm are put aside. In Gal. 3:27 the apostle states that
everyone who is baptized in Christ has put on Christ. Thus, by their
belief, they, as children of God, are new people of the same nature.
In Christ there is no longer Greek nor Jew, neither male nor female,
so too there is no slave or free, "for you are all one in Christ Jesus"
(Gal. 3:28).

For the concrete church on earth, this means that all members
of the church are brothers and sisters in the Lord. The differences
within the brothers and sisters that exist within the church are not
determined by social or occupational position, but by the different

spiritual gifts alone. The spirit creates the order that corresponds to the essence of the church.

THE POSITION WITH RESPECT TO EARTHLY POSSESSIONS

Neither Jesus nor early Christianity developed a social or economic order that required a change in the system of ownership in the world. The vital eschatological expectation ruled out revolutionary action of any kind.

When Jesus demanded complete release from possessions, as in the case of the rich young man, it was for pastoral reasons. For the rich young man who bragged about keeping all of the commandments, there was only one chance for unconditional devotion to God. If he wanted to gain entrance to the kingdom of God and subjugate himself entirely to the lordship of God, he had to give up everything he owned.

Jesus saw in possessions a danger to the inner life of man. He encountered wealth with deep mistrust because he had discovered from experience that it is only with difficulty that the rich man gains entrance to the kingdom of God, for the rich man is given to the illusion that his earthly possessions guarantee the security of his existence. He does not see that what is decisive is not the earthly, but the eternal existence of man. True wealth is wealth in God.

Wealth must not be an end unto itself. It fulfills its task only when it is the means to an end, i.e., when it is used in the service of doing good, for love of one's neighbor. For in this way one accumulates treasure in heaven. When the rich man ignores poor Lazarus lying before his door and denies him all aid, his fate is fulfilled in eternal damnation, from whence there is no escape. Wealth without service to one's brother is service to mammon.

Even though Jesus, with all of his insight into the dangers that wealth posed to the eternal fate of man, did not create a new social and economic order, he did strongly warn his disciples against devoting themselves to the deceit of wealth.

He himself lived entirely free of earthly possessions and he sent the twelve into the cities and villages of Galilee without possessions.

The early church acted according to the ideas of Jesus when it urged the new converts to sell their property and possessions, lands and houses and put the receipts from these sales at the disposal of the apostles, who then distributed them according to need (Acts 2:44; Acts 4:32-37). The daily care of widows, which soon began (Acts 6:1), was also a measure born of social responsibility.

The *church in Antioch* also acted in the spirit of brotherly love after the prophet Agabus had prophesied a famine during the reign of Claudius, when it sent relief to the suffering Christians in Jerusalem and Judea. Each member of the church contributed according to his ability (Acts 11:27-30).

All in all, there was a new approach to property which was determined by the basic demand of Jesus that the task of the disciples was not to lay up treasures on earth, but treasures in heaven (Matth. 6:19-20).

Paul, who himself renounced all earthly possessions, took up a collection for the poor in Jerusalem in order to carry out the resolutions of the council of apostles. This he did with zeal and exemplary faithfulness in the church that he had founded, namely in Macedonia (2 Cor. 8:9). The churches gave according to their means, even above their means, of their own free will (2 Cor. 8:3) and in this way they bore witness to their charity and their solidarity with the "saints" in Jerusalem. Paul sees this collection as an equalizing: "As a matter of equality your abundance at the present time should supply their want, so that their abundance may supply your want, that there may be equality" (2 Cor. 8:14). He states that the service rendered through this gift of love not only relieves the need of the poor, but it also creates a rich spiritual blessing through the many prayers of thanksgiving on the part of the recipients (2 Cor. 9:12). Over and above this one time measure, Paul established the principle that Christians have a duty to do good, especially to those who are of the household of faith (Gal. 6:10). He also emphasized again and again that *pleonexia,* or the desire to possess more, is a sinful pursuit. The Christian should be satisfied with what he has, and should earn his bread by the work of his hand; but he should guard himself from taking advantage of his brother out of a lust for possessions (1 Thessalonians 4:6-11). Christians possessing wealth in this life are admonished in 1 Tim. 6:17-19 not to be haughty and to set their hopes not on the uncertain riches of earthly possessions, but rather on God, to do good, to be rich in good works, and to practice generosity and charity.

Here, too, it turns out that the secular orders of life are not set aside, but the disciples of Jesus are required to put their possessions in the service of love for their brothers and their neighbors.

In addition, the eschatological order is perceptible, which drives certain individual Christians to free themselves completely from earthly possessions in order to serve the gospel fully. In this case, the order of the new age is already realized.

THE FUNDAMENTAL PRINCIPLE OF THE CHURCH

The church of Jesus Christ sees no absolute order in the secular orders of life. The secular orders of life have only relative meaning, for they have validity only in this age.

For this reason Paul demands inner distance from them. This attitude stems from insight into the nature of this age. The life and actions of the Christian belong to the eschatological aspect. Paul formulated this in classical fashion in 1 Cor. 7:29-31: "I mean, brethren, the appointed time has grown very short; from now on, let those who have wives live as though they had none, and those who mourn as though they were not mourning, and those who rejoice as though they were not rejoicing, and those who buy as though they had no goods, and those who deal with the world as though they had no dealings with it. For the form of this world is passing away."

In the words "as if" lie the true relativity of all earthly values and all earthly orders of life. Only with this insight into the true nature of this age can the Christian sustain himself and form his life within the earthly orders of life. If he becomes totally absorbed in the orders of the world, absolutizes it, as does the world, then he gives up his existence as a Christian and shirks his duty toward the order of the new age, which is already reality in Christ and his realm of sovereignty.

CHAPTER FOUR

The Church and the Personal Conduct of the Christian in the World

THE PERSONAL conduct of the Christian in the world has various determining factors.

The decisive concept is the concept of freedom. The freedom of decision according to conscience reflects the non-legalistic gospel. Paul states in Gal. 5:13, "you were called to freedom," and 1 Cor. 3:22 says, "all are yours." The Christian has a sovereign position in the world. He is no longer subject to the forces that he was earlier up against. Through belief in Christ he has become a free man.

From the freedom of conscience it follows that there is no one single way of life for Christians. Since the law has lost all meaning for them, there is no longer any compulsion in the sense that they would be slavishly bound by it. A legalistic control of their life is out of the question.

Decision by conscience is dependent on the measure of faith and the depth of understanding. There are the "strong" and the "weak" in their belief, the immature and the mature Christians, those with a narrow and those with a broad conscience. Paul discussed this in great detail in 1 Cor. 10 (the use of food offered to idols and participation in heathen sacrificial meals) and Romans 14 (vegetarian and non-vegetarian lifestyle). No one has the right to judge the conscience of another. Everyone stands or falls before his own master. Paul is certain that the Christian will stand and not fall, "And he will be upheld, for the Master is able to make him stand" (Rom. 14:4). How much Paul respects the conscience is expressed in the following statement: "One man esteems one day as better than another, while another man esteems all days alike. Let every one be fully convinced in his own mind. He who observes the day, observes it in honor of the Lord. He also who eats, eats in honor of the Lord, since he gives thanks to God; while he who abstains, abstains in honor of the Lord and gives thanks to God" (Rom. 14:5-6). Paul closes with the statement, "So *each of us* shall give account of himself to God" (Rom. 14:12).

Applied to our time, this means that the Christian, as long as he does not serve sin and does not return to the realm of satanic, demonic forces, is free in decisions made through his conscience. It must also be recognized that the decisions of individual Christians can turn out differently.

Let us take as example the position of the Christian toward movies, the theater, art, science—to the realm of cultural activity in general. There are not only gangster films and films that glorify adultery, frivolous plays and suggestive jazz music, not only obscene art, but also films and plays that depict serious problems of life. There is art that serves noble aesthetics and inwardly enriches many people. There is literature that destroys character, but there is also a very valuable body of writing that builds character, increases knowledge, and shows us the heights and depths of human existence. There is not only philosophy and theology that lead us away from God, but also theology that opens to us the wealth of divine revelation and a philosophy that guides us to recognition of eternally valid truths and understanding of reality. What for one person, the "weak" of faith, is a danger and a threat to his inner life, is for the other, the "strong" of faith, an enriching of his spiritual existence.

The one has the freedom to participate in gatherings and events that are an abomination to the other. It is nothing for the one to put on a tuxedo or modern evening dress for an official occasion, while the other would suffer pangs of conscience. Because of conscience, the one leads a narrow bourgeois life. The other, out of inner duty or because of his professional or social position, is broad-minded. The one rejects all cultural activity, while for the other, this is a compelling necessity. There is no single lifestyle for the Christian established by law. The church is not a Jewish synagogue.

But that is only one side of the coin.

The freedom the Christian has is not unlimited or unbridled freedom. For the Christian freedom is a freedom within the commitment to Christ. To the statement, "All things are lawful (to us Christians)," Paul adds, "But not all things are helpful" and "not all things build up," i.e, not everything contributes to the spiritual life (1 Cor. 10:23).

My freedom ends where it begins to impair my inner life and to disturb my community with Christ. My conscience is wrong where it separates me from Christ and leads me back into the world. In other words, my conscience must emanate from my faith. Paul explains in Romans 14:23, "But he who has doubts is condemned, if he eats, because he does not act from faith; for whatever does not proceed from faith is sin." That is, we must never do anything for which we are not completely clear and certain in our responsibility before God. Billy Graham (*Peace with God,* 1954, p. 154) rightly says, "If you have doubt about any particular thing that is bothering you, as to whether it is worldly or not, the best policy is 'don't do it.' "

The First Letter of Peter (2:16) warns us not to use our freedom as a pretext for evil, for as the truly free, we are servants of God. In Gal. 5:13, the statement, "For you were called to freedom" is followed by the exhortation, "Only do not use your freedom as an opportunity for the flesh, but through love be servants of one another." The unlimited use of freedom is not true freedom, for it leads to servitude through the impulses, lusts, passions, and appetites. Only when Christ is Lord of our freedom are we truly free. True freedom is found only in bondage to Christ.

Even though there is no law for the Christian's personal conduct, there are *directions for determining and forming our life.* They are:

•*The words of the Lord.*

Jesus established the order of the lives of his disciples in a clear and unambiguous manner and where Paul has the words of Jesus at his disposal, he treats them as obligatory commandments.

•*The apostle's exhortations of moral responsibility.*

In Romans 12:2 Paul established the basic principle, "Do not be conformed to this world but be transformed by the renewal of your mind, that you may prove what is the will of God, what is good and acceptable and perfect."

Critical judgment, which comes from the renewed spirit and from the conscience that is purified by God, is important. Without sure judgment, given to us by faith, we are not capable of following a clear path.

The fundamental directive of Paul in Romans 12:2 corresponds to other exhortations of the New Testament which are of the greatest significance for us. I emphasize the following:

Romans 13:13-14: "Let us conduct ourselves becomingly as in the day, not in reveling and drunkenness, not in debauchery and licentiousness, not in quarreling and jealousy. But put on the Lord Jesus Christ, and make no provision for the flesh, to gratify its desires."

Eph. 5:10-11: "Try to learn what is pleasing to the Lord. Take no part in the unfruitful works of darkness, but instead expose them." Verses 15-16: "Look carefully then how you walk, not as unwise men but as wise, making the most of the time, because the days are evil." Verse 17: "Understand what the will of the Lord is." Verse 18: "Do not get drunk with wine, for that is debauchery; but be filled with the Spirit."

1 John 2:15-16: "Do not love the world or the things in the world. If anyone loves the world, love for the Father is not in him.

For all that is in the world, the lust of the flesh and the lust of the eyes and the pride of life, is not of the Father but of the world."

2 Cor. 6:14-15: "Do not be mismated with unbelievers. For what partnership have righteousness and iniquity? Or what fellowship has light with darkness? What accord has Christ with Belial? Or what has a believer in common with an unbeliever?"

Philippians 2:14-15: "Do all things without grumbling or questioning, that you may be blameless and innocent, children of God without blemish in the midst of a crooked and perverse generation, among whom you shine as lights in the world."

For the will of God is the holiness of those who believe in Christ. "For God has not called us for uncleanness, but in holiness" (1 Thessalonians 4:7).

The Christian's behavior must correspond to the commitment to a new way of life, assumed during the decision for Christ: "As therefore you received Christ Jesus the Lord, so live in him, rooted and built up in him and established in the faith, just as you were taught" (Col. 2:6-7).

The Letter of James considers pure and undefiled religion as keeping oneself unstained from the world (James 1:27). A very sharp statement that excludes all compromise is found in James 4:4: "Do you not know that friendship with the world is enmity with God? Therefore whoever wishes to be a friend of the world makes himself an enemy of God."

Almost without exception, the passages named contain *imperatives*. They call upon the faithful to lead a life dedicated to God, blessed by him, subjugated to his will. For God, who is holy, wants us to be holy too. We should be perfect, as our heavenly father is perfect (Matth. 5:48). Thus the goal of the imperatives is to put a clear order into our lives, so that we may live according to our calling and according to Christ. Christians who obey the Lord, who died and rose from the dead for them, should separate themselves in their entire being and essence from the world in complete devotion to Christ, cleanse themselves from all impure thoughts and feelings, sanctify their lives, and overcome selfishness through love, so that the all-penetrating, victorious power of redemption will become manifest. Obedience, which is cultivated with the discipline of the Holy Spirit, must encompass all realms of life, including the combating of sins of the tongue, love of self, and greed for money. Above all, however, the admonitions of the New Testament urge us to crucify the flesh and abstain from lust and passions, which are in conflict with the soul (1 Peter 2:11) and impair the activity of the spirit.

The imperatives contain examples of piety that show in a concrete manner what the sanctified life should look like in day-to-day practice. For this reason, the detailed instructions are of help in forming correctly one's existence. They lead to the stagnation of legalistic formalism only when the attempt is made to carry them out without the power of the Holy Spirit. For it is not a question here of a new legality with casuistic individual rules, but a question of orders of life. In the final analysis, they merely serve to develop the one admonition, "Seek sanctification, without which no one can see the Lord." Thus they are meant to show the way in the service of spiritual care where the Christian is unsure in his way of living. They send up signals where ultimate clarity and certainty are lacking. They show the path that must be followed if the goal is to be reached that has been set for us by the call of God (Philippians 3:14). They keep us from transgressing the limits given us and returning to a worldly or even a heathen existence. They set up bounds, so that the opposition between world and church will not be overlooked. The admonitions keep us in the fear of God, in love to Christ, and in the fellowship of the Holy Spirit. Thus they help to maintain the church as the place of Christ's revelation and the instrument of the Holy Spirit. By our fruits we shall be known, for "against such there is no law" (Gal. 5:23).

That the imperatives are not meant legalistically is also shown by the fact that they presuppose the indicative.

Christians should lead a holy life because they are holy. They should crucify their flesh along with their lusts and passions because they are crucified with Christ. They should break the chains that hold them to the earth because they have broken the grip of sin and transgression. They should live a new life because they are new people—dead, buried, and resurrected with Christ in baptism. Within the facts established by God, which are the content of the indicative, lies at the same time the reason why the fulfillment of the demands and admonitions of the imperative is possible. The indicative is the power of the imperative. Thus, the imperative is the means of divine grace to form our life in such a way that it corresponds to an existence renewed by atonement, faith, baptism, and reception of the spirit. Through the imperative, the indicative should be put into practice.

We also need firm order in our personal lives and in the life of the church because otherwise we would be in danger of building from the freedom we have in Christ a self-chosen way of life that abandons the path of obedience toward the revealed will of God. Everywhere in the life of the church, the concept of order plays a decisive role. If our moral life is not in order, then our spiritual life is also out of order. Being under the lordship of Christ means adapting ourselves to the order given us by God, for that alone is the healing order that sustains and keeps us in grace and love. W. Grün says quite rightly, "The ultimate reasons for the breakdown of order point to serious internal deficiencies. That is namely the great calamity of our times: the loss or lack of substance of our piety. Are there not already too many among us who no longer know the New Testament's experience of salvation, who have had no experience with the Holy Spirit and do not want to have any? We clearly state: He who knows nothing of a breach in his life will also know nothing and will want to know nothing of commitment to the new order and will want to know nothing of the succour and blessing from the orders and rules of our piety."[1]

•*The example of the apostle.*

Paul indicated repeatedly that, by the grace of God, he was capable of leading a life of sanctification. For this reason, he could invite the churches to imitate him (Philippians 3:17 and others) and take him as their example (1 Cor. 4:16) as he, in turn, was the imitator of Christ (1 Cor. 11:1). Paul, as the pardoned servant of

---

[1]W. Grun, *Ordnung und Ordnungen in unserer Frömmigkeit.* "Die Gemeinde" No. 14, 10 July 1955, p. 212.

God, was able to say of himself, "For our boast is this, the testimony
of our conscience that we have behaved in the world, and still more
toward you, with holiness and godly sincerity, not by earthly wisdom
but by the grace of God" (1 Cor. 10:31-33). From this he derives the
right to say admonishingly, "Do all to the glory of God. Give no offense to Jews or to Greeks or to the church of God, just as I try to
please all men in everything I do, not seeking my own advantage,
but that of many, that they may be saved."

Our way of life must be such that we do not prevent people
from coming to the faith. That is a decisive motivation for shaping
our entire existence. For it often happens that a person who is
deeply touched by the proclaimed word is repelled because he takes
offense at the behavior of those who confess faith in Christ. Or he
may have come to the living faith in Christ, been added to the
church, and then experienced a great disappointment when he saw
that among many members of the church word and deed did not
correspond to pious behavior and ethical acts.

If we are not examples, but offend non-believers and those who
are not firm in their faith, we assume the guilt. Jesus himself warned
us not to offend our brother or our neighbor. The most poignant
expression of this is the statement of Jesus in Mark 9:42: "Whoever
causes one of these little ones who believe in me to sin, it would be
better for him if a great millstone were hung round his neck and he
were thrown into the sea."

•*The pastoral service that is rendered us in the clarification of
the concrete questions of our lives.*

Here we give the word of Billy Graham *(Peace with God,* pp.
152-54), "The world has a tendency to lead us into sin—evil companions, pleasures, fashions, opinions, and aims of the world.

"You will find in your born-again experience that your pleasures have been lifted into an entirely new and glorious realm. Many
non-Christians have accused the Christian life as being a set of rules,
taboos, vetoes, and prohibitions. This is another lie of the Devil. It is
not a series of 'don'ts,' but a series of 'dos.' You become so busy in the

work of Christ and so completely satisfied with the things of Christ that you do not have time for the things of the world."

And then Billy Graham comes to the personal problems of life.

"Many young people come and ask me, 'Is this wrong?' or 'Is that wrong?' One simple question, earnestly and prayerfully asked, will settle about ninety percent of your problems along this line. Just ask this question to yourself every time, 'What would Christ have me to do?' Another question you can ask is, 'Can I ask His blessing upon this particular thing for me?' 'What would Christ think about my amusements, recreation, books, companions, and television programs?' We cannot compromise or bargain here. There must be an out-and-out stand for Christ.

"It does not mean that in society we are snobs or have a superiority complex, lest we be in danger of spiritual pride—which would be far worse than any worldliness. But today there are so many professing Christians who are walking hand in hand with the world that you cannot tell the difference between the Christian and the sinner. This should never be.

"The Christian should stand out like a sparkling diamond against a rough background. He should be more wholesome than anyone else. He should be poised, cultured, courteous, gracious, but firm in the things that he does and does not do. He should laugh and be radiant, but he should refuse to allow the world to pull him down to its level."

But with all this, the question of the powers that shape our lives is not yet answered completely. If the law is no longer in effect, then what is to take its place? To this, the apostle Paul answers: *the Holy Spirit.*

Christians are people of the spirit. They have received the spirit of God. God put the Holy Spirit into their hearts (1 Thess. 4:8). He has "poured (it) out upon us richly through Jesus Christ our Saviour" (Titus 3:6). The spirit lives within the believers. Their body is a temple of the Holy Spirit. Just as they are under the lordship of Christ, they are also under the leadership of the spirit.

From this comes their obligation to live no longer according to the flesh, but through the spirit, to put to death the impulses of the body (Rom. 8:12).

Everything depends on our devoting ourselves to the power of the Holy Spirit. The more we do that, the more we will overcome the spirit of the world and bear the fruits of the spirit.

Organic vital functions emerge from life in the spirit. Through the Holy Spirit, the groundwork of our existence has been changed, for the Holy Spirit is a power that transforms hearts and lives. Through the Holy Spirit, our lives are repeatedly dedicated to God and Christ is transfigured in us.

The Holy Spirit leads us to all truth. It provides us with knowledge that surpasses the bounds of human reason. "For the Spirit searches everything, even the depths of God" (1 Cor. 2:10).

The Holy Spirit makes us firm in our faith and in love. It causes Christ to take form in us (Gal. 4:19) and causes us, in the innermost part of our existence, to be changed from one degree of glory to another (2 Cor. 3:17-18).

The more we live in the spirit, the more clearly and distinctly we will be able to shape our lives according to the instructions of the spirit. For our sanctification is the work of the Holy Spirit, not the result of legal demands that we ourselves or others set up. If the Holy Spirit is the determining factor in our lives, then we are capable of recognizing and doing the will of God.

In the final analysis, the question of the relationship between church and world is solved in the concrete problems of our lives through the Holy Spirit.

In living according to the spirit, our redemption with regard to our personal way of life is accomplished. For only where the spirit of the Lord is, is there freedom: the freedom from the law, which is at the same time the strongest and deepest bondage to Christ.

The Holy Spirit makes us joyous children of God, sure of salvation, liberated from the law of sin and death, who are also free from all confinement and stagnation. For the Holy Spirit is a spirit that creates life. It makes us into living people, creating out of the fullness of the spirit. Through it, we travel a safe path, victorious in the battle with the world.

We come now to the final point of our discussion.

We began with the concept of freedom and the personal conscience of the Christian and saw that there is freedom only in bondage to Christ and that possession of the spirit obliges the Christian to live according to the spirit.

However, this does not tell the whole story; for the Christian never stands alone. He must make the decision of his conscience in responsibility to God, but *the question is whether or not, in each case, he can realize this decision.*

Just as the Christian is bound to Christ, he is also bound to the church. In the church however, as we have seen, there are people with various degrees of faith and knowledge. The Christian is in the fellowship of the brothers and Paul's supreme principle is that the church is built in love, that its unity should not be destroyed, and that the conscience of a brother should not be offended. Thus arises the question that moves Paul most profoundly: What am I to do, I who am strong in my faith and knowledge, when my brother who is weak in his faith, cannot share the decision of my conscience?

There are *two possibilities.*

One is that I act without regard to my brother, who is narrow-minded in his conscience. In this case I am justified in myself, but I offend the commandment of love. My brother who is weaker in his faith is offended by my action and my manner of shaping my life in the freedom given to me. To be sure, I can try to make my position clear to him and raise him to my level of perception, but this will be successful only in rare instances. As a rule, however, if I have my way completely, I trouble the conscience of the other person and destroy the community of the church and endanger its unity. In this case, I sin against my brother, the community, and thereby against Christ as well who, after all, also died for the brother who is weaker in faith (1 Cor. 8:12).

The other possibility is that I sacrifice my personal decision in favor of my brother and the church and forgo that which, in itself, is permissible to me. The decision of my conscience, which I can justify completely, is then limited by the conscience of my brother. This is what Paul demands. Thus, the sacrifice is to be made not by the one who is weak in faith, but the one who is strong. The tie to the community sets a limit to my freedom.

Paul knew quite well the necessity involved in this solution of the problem. In 1 Cor. 10:29-30, he formulates the objections, which he understands quite well, in the question of the rightness or wrongness of eating food offered to idols: "Why should my liberty be determined by another man's scruples? If I partake with thankfulness, why am I denounced because of that for which I give thanks?" But Paul says, "If someone says to you, 'This has been offered in sacrifice,' then out of consideration for the man who informed you, and for conscience's sake—I mean his conscience, not yours—do not eat it" (1 Cor. 10:29-30).

Paul on his part, although his personal conscience dictates otherwise, comes to the conclusion, "Therefore, if food is a cause of my brother's falling, I will never eat meat, lest I cause my brother to fall" (1 Cor. 8:13).

Paul sacrificed his freedom for the sake of his brother and for the unity of the church. He perceived this sacrifice as minor in comparison with the sacrifice Christ made for us through his death.

Paul teaches us this: In following Christ, I must forgo my right, if love of my brother demands it. For the sake of the church, the individual must under certain circumstances forgo fulfillment of the decision of his conscience, even though it is completely justified. Christ and the church must be at the center of the action. The church is bigger and more important than the individual and his freedom. It is on this principle that all problems of personal conduct and lifestyle are to be solved for the person who lives in the church of Christ and affirms that church.

Church and World in the New Testament!

We have given attention to the following thoughts:

1. The church is separate from the world.
2. The church is placed in the world.
3. In its action, the church is in a state of tension which is eschatologically determined.
4. The church no longer lives under the law but under grace.

5. Every Christian is free in the decisions of his conscience, but the Christian's freedom is only possible in bondage to Christ and to the church. Christ, the Holy Spirit, and the conscience of our brother establish the limitations to our individualistic self-assertion. Love that is willing to sacrifice is the law and regulator of all ethical action.

The Author

JOHANNES SCHNEIDER was born in Stadtoldenhorf, 23 September 1895. He earned his D. Rer. Pol. from Göttingen in 1922, his Lic. Theol. from Berlin in 1927. He was appointed instructor at the University of Berlin in 1930, professor in 1935, and was appointed professor at Humboldt University (Berlin) in 1950. After World War II Professor Schneider was reappointed to his post at Berlin where he became dean of the theological faculty, the only Baptist in the divinity school. He was the author of eighteen books including *Der Hebräerbrief* (ET: *The Letter to the Hebrews*), and contributed thirty-one articles to the *Theologisches Wörterbuch zum Neuen Testament*. Professor Schneider died 23 May 1970.

The Translators

HENLEE BARNETTE was for twenty-six years Professor of Christian Ethics at Southern Baptist Theological Seminary, and is now Clinical Professor in the Department of Psychiatry and Behavioral Sciences, University of Louisville School of Medicine. His *Introducing Christian Ethics* (1961), a popular textbook, has gone through seven editions and has been translated into several languages. *Exploring Medical Ethics* (Mercer University Press, 1982) was his eleventh book.

WAYNE BARNETTE studied in Vienna, Munich, Stockholm, and Lund. At Lund he earned the degree Filosofie Kandidat in Russian-German. He taught Russian at Vanderbilt University and earned his Ph.D. from Vanderbilt in 1979. He is now a professional translator of Slavic languages in Nashville.

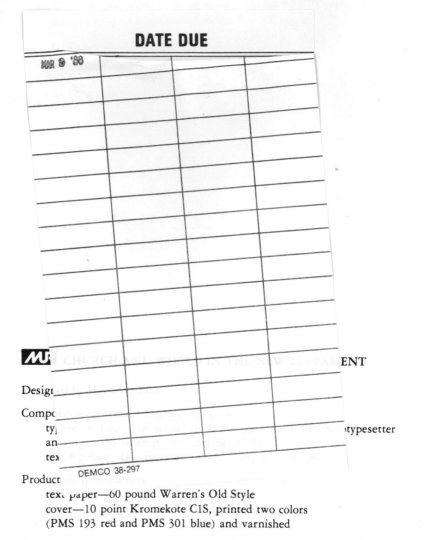

DATE DUE

MAR 9 '88

DEMCO 38-297

THE CHURCH AND WORK IN THE NEW TESTAMENT

Design...

Compo...
  ty... ...typesetter
  an...
  te...

Product...
  text paper—60 pound Warren's Old Style
  cover—10 point Kromekote C1S, printed two colors
  (PMS 193 red and PMS 301 blue) and varnished

Printing (offset lithography) and binding by Omnipress of Macon, Inc.,
  Macon, Georgia